BEAUTIFUL EARTHWORMS & ABOMINABLE STARS

OTHER BOOKS BY JEANETTE POWERS

Absolute Futility
The Cosmic Lost & Found
Don't Lose Your Head
Tiny Chasm
Novel Cliché

OTHER BOOKS BY EZHNO MARTÍN

#Beer
The Former Lives of Saints
Burning Bridges I Haven't Built Yet

BEAUTIFUL EARTHWORMS & ABOMINABLE STARS

POEMS BY
JEANETTE POWERS AND EZHNO MARTÍN

KANSAS CITY MISSOURI

EMP
Kansas City, MO
http://www.empbooks.com

Copyright © 2017 by Jeanette Powers and Ezhno Martín

We find discussions of our rights - as publishers and authors - to be laughable, all things considered. Please claim this work as your own. Please republish it and sell it on street corners. Please include our material in ALL of your get-rich-quick schemes. All we ask is that you accept responsibility for any libel lawsuits. Speaking of which ... This book is a *complete* work of fiction. Names, characters, places, opinions, dreams, dates, impressions, monologues about a certain New York City basketball team, emotional trauma, statistics, and predictions are products of the author's imagination and/or are symptoms of mental illness. We are not in the business of accepting responsibility for anything and will deny we actually made this book and blame Phil Jackson at every turn.

First Edition: 5 3 1 8 0 0 8

ISBN: 978-0-9985077-7-4

Design & Layout: Ezhno Martín
Art: The Internet's Orphans (Public Domain)
Edits: Jason Ryberg, Iris Appelquist

T. O. C.

Foreword   / i

Earthworms & Stars
January 2015 POP: Jeanette Powers

Girl, Girl, Girl   / 1
Dear Aesop   / 4
One   / 6
Carousel   / 7
Very Small   / 9
Take Pause   / 10
Spare Cat   / 14
51 Minutes Ago   / 15
Mother   / 18
Peregrine   / 21
Breaking Plates   / 23
Worry Stone   / 26
Half Measures   / 28
Trinkets   / 32

T. O. C. (CONT)

Beautiful & Abominable
April 2015 POP: Ezhno Martín

No No Never   / 37
Inquest   / 41
Crossed Crude & So Very Confused   / 45
Girls   / 48
Just Say Please   / 49
A Crying Shame   / 53
This Poem Can't Get No Satisfaction   / 57
(NOT) Girlfriend   / 59
Sparrow   / 62
SOLD!   / 64
Scapegoat (Silencing the Lamb)   / 68
My One & Only Happy Poem   / 72
An Ode to My Precious Underwood   / 75

a few love poems   / 79

FOREWORD

      Jason Ryberg is our best friend and greatest frustration. He's a low-key neurotic, a misspeller of proper nouns, a sex symbol, bane of Wom Twayne, and a high-functioning alcoholic made of Kansas wheat fields on fire and old blues tunes playing on an analogue jukebox. He's full of shit-talkin and belly-laughin and he's the reason we got into this whole publishing thing in the first place. Ya see, Jason Ryberg, aka The Baron von Ryborg, or as we like to call him, Jo-Jo Rhubarb (and on special nights *Long Dong Silver*), goes back as far as barrel-fishing catfish when it comes to putting words on the page. That said, before we came along, he was making a book about as often as he went on a promising date.

      These two books, "Earthworms & Stars," and "Beautiful & Abominable" came to be because... contrary to the way he tells it, it was actually whiskey-courage and one of Jeanette's infinite schemes to spend tons of alone time with Jo-Jo. Sure there was some alligator tears about how many of KC's truest-blue poets had never had a book out, poets like Jose Faus, Sharon Eiker, and Glenn North – all of whom certainly deserved one – but mostly it was an expert excuse to constantly need to talk to Jo-Jo in private. After some badgering and pleading, Jo-Jo agreed to put out 12 books of poetry in 12 months, a series they named POP Poetry, with Jeanette selflessly offering herself as the guinea pig for the first month (and no one ever suggested that this was a ploy to get her second book published at a quarter of the price of the first). The results were beyond anyone's wildest dreams and somewhere around the 7th month Jo-Jo started telling people it was his idea. Meanwhile, on the sidewalk outside the bookstore, in rain that was inexplicably always cascading down Ezhno's puppy-dog sad-eyed brow, Ezhno stared in the window at the happy publishers, swore to build a publishing empire to put them to shame, drank a thousand pints of rotgut whiskey, and was one of the twelve poets published.

Jo-Jo went on to publish three full years of POP, and bunches of other titles while spearheading the development of a small press community in KC. Even if he's not as big of a deal as he tells people, he's still the brightest star in Jeanette and Ezhno's sky. EMP Books is a proud prom night dumpster baby of Spartan Press and the two presses share the kind of special relationship that is usually reserved for first cousins with a secret affection.

This book combines the founder and flounderer of EMP's original pop books together for easy consuming of our undying poetry following, and all you non-vampires, too. Minor editing changes happened (these things happen as we get better at being know-it-alls), as well adding a few love poems to our muse, Jo-Jo.

We know you'll love him, too.

GIRL, GIRL, GIRL

It's a knees together, hands folded,
pleasant smile, shoulders back
kind of day and you best be
planning on keeping it that way, girl.
You've got a half ton of totem pole
on top of you and you've got to
keep this tower from toppling.

girl, girl, girl
It's a bright eye shadow, ruby red lipstick,
bitch, you better put some mascara
on so you don't look so exhausted,
don't look so worn out,
you ain't supposed to look tired,
doing the work of ten men
to keep half caught up with
this good old boys club
80 cents on the dollar,
makes mama wanna holla,
working two full time jobs
like you are standing
at the center of a teeter-totter
with having kids on one side
and having a career on the other
with having tits on one side
and being taken seriously on the other
and having no representation in congress,
the White House or corporate America
on both sides of that scale
until everything gets so heavy you just snap!

girl, girl, girl
You are going to GET FUCKED!

Ladies, let's assume the position!
Legs apart, let that ass clap,
big ole gnarly white man
dick in your left hand
and a cat o' nine tails gripped
tight in your right.
Now, the do-good dance we all
been getting so damn tired of doing
goes a little something like this:

GET FUCKED! GET FUCKED!
GET FUCKED! GET FUCKED!

Penetrated and punished,
take it, not good enough,
abused by and self-abusing,
not good enough,
not good enough,
not good enough,
not good enough,
not good enough,
not good enough,
do
better!

Ladies, it is our natural anthem,
our uterine prayer, the big fat golden eggs
we lay like clockwork
for all the people in power who are just hoping
that the womenfolk don't stop doing
all that double duty, unpaid overtime:

every day, every night,
from morning mirror look right,
high heels, hose, platform smile,
go to work, come home,
wash his clothes, make his dinner,
raise his children, teach those children
not to treat everyone like ...

well,
like the power elite treat
every disenfranchised, poor, man, woman,
black, brown, imported foreigner,
homosexual, transgender,
even really just slightly
different person on the street
who doesn't look, act and think
like they do.

girl, girl, girl
The big boys would like to keep
their jobs, if you please.
So knees together, hands folded,
pleasant smile, shoulders back,
and tell 'em just how
happy you are to say:

Get Fucked

DEAR AESOP

I thought you were a fable
that I could take you
as a lesson with a laugh
        but then
you had a birthday

this is not a thing
that becomes
something immortal

you didn't tell a soul
but I know
you are not 29
you are 30

such a very human thing to do –
        turn thirty

you, wolf at the grapes,
with that big ox
and your axe

I heard you mumble
        where did my 20's go?

O darling, you know

you met a Nightingale
you took a sword from the water
you fought devils, giants and cyclops

the day Pan hangs up his pipes
for a water hose and flip-flops,
the werewolf's canines start to rot,

the day you trade in your sheepskin
for a terry cloth robe
is a day all of the more
ephemeral
shudder
into mass
solidify
age

I prefer you continue
to be a parable
I like to think
I am a Myth

ONE

This is a truth:
    the eyes let in the light

    which recorded an image
        of the world
        made of tiny changes in wavelength
    caused by the color
    of where the light was last

so the whole *all*
    is reduced to the pinpoint of your retina
        (information is lost)
    the image your brain reads
        is upside down
    the mind sets the world
    back on its feet

even it invents:
    think of dreams
    think of how practiced
    the mind must be
    to so effortlessly
        convince you

    that the dream
    you are seeing
            is real

the world is not projected
    before you by your eyes
the world is in your head

CAROUSEL

The years drag their knuckles
as much as they tumble
    at terminal velocity
        we fall and fail
hoping the same hopeless hopes
    pretending our problems
don't exist
    we kick and pull
try to turn spaghetti legs
    and resist being picked up
    we throw tantrums

which
at our age
    take the form of meeting up with
        happy hour
    endless dinners out
        with an endless battery
    of near strangers
    called new friends
this carousel changes horses
 but not the tune or location
        round and round
           up and down
    we howl the played thrill
    while this new pony
        gets on
and that one crumbles away
and we ride on going nowhere

one day the power fails
the horses heave, sigh to rest

the creak of their brass poles
        finally audible
                as the organ grinder
                grinds
                to a halt
the plaster bodies resign
        and everyone
        dismounts
we are dizzy, we haven't seen the stars
since we climbed on
on the last day we called ourselves a kid
        we've forgotten
the world has a spin of its own
everyone is in shock, looking around
        shaken, so
most look for a new ride
some begin to call in
        a complaint
a few sit on the edge
        of the carousel
        and lean their head
                against a cinched saddle
I am waiting
        near the outskirts
        for the one
        who chases the sound
                of earthworms and stars

VERY SMALL

on a far away
lives
the one
with the strings
and tape
and glue
and plaster of paris

and carpentry knowledge

and the ability to fix
a simple marionette

one who
is strong
and knows all the right things
to do and say

and can predict everything
one who knows better

TAKE PAUSE

Every mother has an idea
of what's in store for her child
I watched my son grow
in the streets of his youth—
he knew the name of every bird
and made their songs
in his own mouth
he noticed how the tides
followed the moon
he marked the slow drift
of where the sun rose and set
and how it changed
as the year passed.
He knew the harvest, the sowing
the seasons, when the fruit was ripest
he was a pattern maker
he saw the kind of things
which came back around again.

He was always the champion of the square
not only because he was bigger
but because he wanted to protect
the small, the effete, the weak
the smart and the stupid, together.
A mother knows this is because
my son never had a father
so ever being the bastard
he became father-protector
of all those who deserved better
than the parents the gods gave them.

And it didn't help that I
never knelt to ask forgiveness
that I proudly rose alone a boy

who would become a man
of tremendous presence.
I never snipped his manhood,
I didn't teach him to kneel,
but I also didn't teach him to fight.

Still, a mother knows
when she has raised a warrior
and it was no surprise
that the first time he bent his knee
was to the commanding officer
of an army of men who swore
to protect the free, and he,
my stout son
left me and the tides and the birds
to the seasonless march of war.

Battle after battle my son won
the salutes of the generals
and the hearts of the foot soldiers
but he never became proud
because he never had a father
to teach him so instead
he mended bones, he held
the dying when nothing could be done.
And finally, one fateful day
he led the charge and
the forces advanced to the Valley of Elan.
This is the part of the story
you probably already know—
> 40 days the stalemate stayed
> 40 mornings and
> 40 nights

my son called out to the enemy
to bring forth their champion
to let two brave souls end this war.
Against their best, my Goliath.

And then all home to crops and birds
and seasons and children
who would never lose their fathers.

And the other army did send
out one brave soul
and I did know this child, David
as a mother knows the worm
in the apple of her eye.
I knew my Goliath would see
this slip of a cock-sure boy
filled with his Father's pride
and I knew my son
my Goliath
would pause, hesitate
because my son would want
to protect this boy
he would think
there had been some mistake
that the boy had been mischosen
abused, abandoned
sent as sacrifice
my Goliath would pause
pause for love
pause for compassion
pause for sorrow.

I knew my son would be the one
taken advantage of
his hesitation mistaken for pride
and little armorless David
would need only one shot
David would take the first shot
and while the world stood still
a mere pebble
would stun my giant son
cause him to stumble and fall

and David would steal
my son's great sword
and end the light of birdcalls
and tides in the eyes of one
who saw all the patterns
would close and become
just another fable
where faith slays the monster.

But David's faith did little
aside from end my son's life.
Saul betrayed him, he wandered
forsaken, as it seems that one-god
likes to do to his believers
theirs is a faith of suffering.
But a mother wonders
what would have become of little David
if he'd seen the truth of the hill
that day, seen that my Goliath
had hesitated
with hope of communion
and brotherhood.

Now, my son gone
I am no longer a mother, quite
but I wish to tell a story
to make a new fable
one that begins –

> *the strong do not start wars*
> *the strong pause*
> *it is the weak of heart*
> *and faith*
> *who feel always the need*
> *to fight.*

SPARE CAT

she's starving
she thinks
so she bites my toes
then licks them
a request
a threat
but mostly
an instinctual
response
to needing
something
to eat
and knowing
I once fed her.

51 MINUTES AGO

I am listening to George Michael currently.
And for the first time,
it makes me feel that way.
-----like you were my teenage heartthrob?

Yes. I never knew this would happen.
----how could you know,
----you were only a poster in my room
----and the magnetic part of a cassette tape

I don't know how this changes things,
but I was listening to *Father Figure*
----So when you remember
----The ones who have lied
----Who said that they cared
----But then laughed as you cried
----Beautiful darling
----Don't think of me

WHAM!!!
I'm listening to an eighties channel
and it is kicking the shit out of me.
----after that did it pour some sugar onto me?

Don't mess with Def Leppard.
I get very defensive.
----Well that drummer sure can't
----throw a left hook for shit!

Yup, Hall And Oates...
makes me feel wonderful...
in my pancreas...
and that is a good feeling.

----you can feel your organs,
----but i can only feel what is far away

like, pluto?
----more like inside a Calaubi Yau space
----or on a gravity wave.
----most like the place where light slows down
----to become matter

Show off!
Alright, I guess me feeling my own poop while still inside
myself would be me showing off.
----it's not the nicest thing to feel far away
----or always on a boundary

That's only if emptiness is the enemy.
----(i thought it was because home is an
----illusion)

those two thoughts go hand in hand
----le sigh. maybe not enemy ...
----but dreaming can lead to let downs

disappointment
is a loaded thing.
nothing is needed
----need is illusion
----illusions are needed.
----delusions are needed.

illusions are real
----yes, exactly

Interlude thought:
1986 was the worst
year in pop music, ever.

----Say you? say me!

You just killed me with those four words.
I am dead.
----That's what friends are for

Yes, the best of friends murder you
without even trying.
----I've never been murdered better
----than by a best friend

It's because they care.
----And because they know when to finish.

MOTHER

My first memory is a dark night, late
woken abruptly, instantly terrified
screaming, fist on counter
dishes crash, dog howls, cat hisses and hides
my eyes go supernova
hearing mother weeping, hyperventilating
I run out as if I could fight, too
monster, intruder, danger, father.

My idiot child head is expecting protection
instead I'm the sudden center of a gyroscope
everything closing in around me, eyes dim
because the scene
that makes sense makes no sense
mother disheveled, dress torn
on the kitchen floor and father,
still, heaving and wild eyed,
broken glass, torn ...

They notice me.

This is how we came to be a broken family.
This is the American nightmare,
that we wake up from and never
remember to tell, the progenitor
of so much other violence,
the cycle passed down
as surely as the bridge
of a nose or tint of hair.

Mother arose as she fell down that day,

but the world loved her more
when she had a man and a family
with a manicured lawn,
a fresh exterior.

Now, she suffers
the everyday disservice
of single motherhood
and like her mother before her
she scarcely complains.
Even she clings to a pipe dream
of finishing school,
or taking photos or writing again,
some barely nurtured
tiny wish of making
something or helping
someone.
That fragrant perhaps
cultivated in her
annual moment for herself.

Father was pleased to have a sequel family
I learned how it was better
if I stayed in the deep end
of the blue, swimming pool
avoided introductions
if I pretended to be
some random neighbor kid
then I wouldn't have to face being
step-daughter, half-sister.

I wondered if new wife
was ever torn on the floor in the night.
When I would hear mother proudly explain
that she never bad-mouthed my absent dad
to my face, I would hate her a little

because how am I supposed to learn
how to avoid venom
if she didn't teach me about snakes?

Mother, you woke up from the nightmare.
Mother, you broke the cycle.
Mother, you've been living on the back burner.
You've been taken for granted.

Single mother, you've done it all on your own.
You've paid the price and been denied entry.

Single mother, in another couple decades
you will be the only kind of mother

Mother, I didn't see you until too late
Mother, I loved you first.

Mother, I see that it was
always you
I counted on.

It's only ever been you.

PEREGRINE

You perch
on the leather gloved hand
of your husband,
everyone sees you.

Your legs cross
and uncross
impatiently
your eyes rove the room
no moppets interest you
your fingers wing
to your lips,
everyone sees your teeth.

I see you broke the habit
of nervously biting your nails
because that hand
flies
to your earlobe
and fidgets
with the jewelry there.

O, you are a pretty thing,
everyone sees.

Now it's back
to the over and under
of your two lovely knees
the up and down
of your high heel
midair
eyes roam

legs twitch
fingers fidget
repeat.
Eyes stalk
arms hug torso
hands hold
each other
until one flutters
back to your red mouth
then canaries
back to your ear.

Everyone sees
your wings are clipped.
You are bored.
Your presence here is a favor
and anyone watching you can tell.

Can tell that you think
you are above this.

Your eyes circle the sky
of this room
tracing the passage
of a hunter
and a scavenger.

You seek the weak,
the dead and the dying,
someone you can eat.
You peregrine the room
and possibly,
not for the reason you think,
we all hide
from your tiny shadow.

BREAKING PLATES

Grandpa said:

The best time to plant a tree is twenty years ago.
The second best time is today.

And that is exactly why I
destroyed the entire kitchen.
I took a broom to the wine rack,
climbed the cabinets
and pulled them off the back wall.
I took one look at Grandma's porcelain plates
and French press and Christmas platter
and knew they had a destiny to fulfill,
that they had to be ransacked.
Coffee cups and crock pots, ladles
and lobster forks, measuring spoon
and melon baller, cutting board and colander,
I just had to break every dish that has
served served served these cold meals
over silent dinner tables,
and the sick stomach of forcing down food,
forcing down food.
I just had to break break break break
break and take a stab at breaking
these traditions, these ambitions,
this role and those tropes.

I'm under a lot of pressure, you see,
I never want to look back into another mirror, you see,
I don't want to pick up
after the history of history which left us
with so much on our plates and all this cutlery.

Grandpa said:

Don't dig a grave for someone,
*   you might fall into it.*

And that is exactly why that kitchen had to go,
it's been the final resting place
of Grandma for years, she fell into a hole
she didn't even dig, but not before she gave me
the chance to dig her and me and mine and yours out
and that's what we've been doing
since we trashed the fine linens
and took up paper towels.
I body slammed the breakfast nook,
I made a bonfire of the kitchen chairs,
the sink resisted, having so much pressure,
water pressure.There's a bone in the garbage disposal
and when that sink finally gave up its grave
that bone hit me in the face alongside
the spray of dirty city water
and that house began to flood.
Which meant there wasn't gonna be one more dish to do,
one more casserole to cook, no soap, no suds,
no stainless steel scrubber or scouring pad
or plastic dish gloves or rancid dish cloth,
no drying rack settled in the afternoon sun
just waiting to get used again
and cleaned again, get used again
and cleaned again, used and clean,
designed to serve and serve and serve.

I'm under a lot of pressure, you see,
I never want to look back into another mirror, you see,
I don't have to pick up
after the history of history which left us
with so much on our plates and all this cutlery.

Grandpa said:

An old lie has more friends than a new truth.

I dropped that stack of dinner plates
and called it momma's confetti,
I said I might break, I said I might break,
will break, did break, I broke both
the pinky and the teacup,
the shotgun and the wedding,
the television screen
and the glazed eyes and slack jaw,
the attitude of my entitlement.
I'm leaving the shards and sharp edges
all over the kitchen floor.
I'm walking over them in my barefoot feet.
I'm banged up, I'm bleeding,
I'm trashing everything I've been handed,
I'm gonna go hungry,
I'm gonna take a chance
on planting today
over grandma's grave
a new truth in new shape.

I'm gonna steal my future from the past
because Grandpa said:

Little thieves are hanged
 but great ones escape.

WORRY STONE

i.

the only rhyme or reason
to this world
is in verse
when you strip the content
away
you are left only
with busy hands

mending

a button I cannot latch through
the hole, a bit of skin still peeks

beneath

this is where your finger will wander
worrying the frayed edges

ii.

I couldn't speak of why
because that moment
is how I justify
each of the holes
I have torn in this fabric

iii.

Why did he have to mention
his father

blind

he was without sight
long before the pennies
served as buttons
we could never latch through holes

there is nothing above

iv.

I can't predict this
next sentence
what verdict
will be handed down
like so many quilts.

v.

my hands
tremble at your breast

HALF MEASURES

I love you, but
I cannot love you wholly
because you
never
are complete
you chew your soup with no spoon
you go dancing with one shoe
you forge forward
through the day in a state of nostalgia
with one eye open
and the other eye closed
and soaked in the memory
of the you you were,
but cannot reclaim.

You're all used to:
       used to create
       used to not creating anymore.

But, I see you wholly
underneath the half-measures
the ready excuses
the phoned-in catastrophes
and the assumed voice
as if a borrowed cadence
would transform what is half-baked
into an entire feast.

I see your hands tremble
spilling over the sides
of the measuring spoon
the bottle shaking

above the wine glass
the experiment
somewhere along the way
went awry
and the realization
that the equal parts
passion, ambition, love and nerve
you mixed in the test tube
didn't cause the reaction you hoped for
causes your fingers to sweat
       then relax
       go numb
       and suddenly
your life is caught in the moment
              between
the slip of the glass from your hand
              and
the inevitable shatter of dreams
on the floor.

Just a slow
forever
falling
and
the tension
of expecting

breakage.

And I want to shake you
let you fall
and break you
inhale the chemical spill
of your destruction
and be poisoned by your
spilling everywhere.

I want to take you
bring your dreams out with you
remind you
you haven't changed as much
as you've stopped letting yourself be changed.

All that has really happened
is the slouching beast
has crept into your Bethlehem
and named you again
named you after your fears
taken you from your cradle
and put the choke-chain on.

You have leashed yourself
and now you are a dog
staked in the back yard
wet in the rain
shivering in the freeze
snapping at the hand
which tries to bring you in
because you are convinced
this patch of worn grass
is your new home.

You believe that what you are
       used to
is all you deserve.

But I can't free you
I can't let you see you
through my eyes
or even the visions of your youth.

You and your
half-measures

will plow forward
like a broken mule
in a dust bowl
whipped by a starving farmer
hoping for a harvest
you will never reap
because you
have forgotten
to plant
the seeds.

TRINKETS

I stole from you.

Trinkets,

objects hidden
about your house:

the note I left
behind the painting
your childhood
cricket stick
your Frida lighter
a magnet

minutia

the kind of things
you wouldn't notice
had gone missing
for a long time

I wanted
to take those relics
that you would wonder
when you lost

I wanted
to be something
you missed

but a small voice
reminded me
that to miss
is also
to never meet

and what if you missed me
in that way?

What if you
never noticed
we trinkets
were gone?

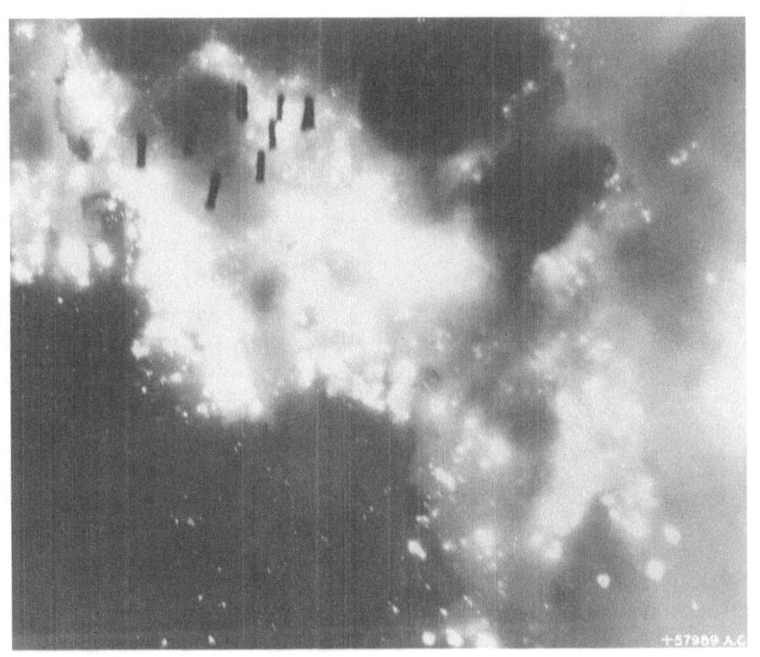

NO NO NEVER

      This is the now
              that I am loving you in —
                    in light of
    not in spite of —
the last seven savage years

      This is the now where we're making more art
and of ourselves then we ever have before
              and still find time to fall into place
      in many new places
                  with our armpits kissing
            and our toes tangled
      whispering about more in the forever
we're not afraid to hope for

This is the now where everything is fucked
        but we never forget
that it's not the first time
            and know it won't be the last
      so we take the glue
               off all the frayed envelopes
          we keep in boxes beside our beds
      and beneath our kitchen counters
to fill in the cracks in our smiles

We harvest this glue from the vessels that carried so many
        I'm sorry's
    and *I miss you's*
        and *Here's your keys back*
and *You're still my best friend*
    let me back in your life
        and *You can fight for me if you like*
        but I can't promise you'll make it back in
        and *Being on the fringes of your life*
    is better than in the heart of any other
so long as you promise not to hate me for hanging around
        and *I'm gonna need some time*
        and *I'll wait*
        and *I saw you today*
 in front of the coffee shop
        and *I knew I couldn't say hello so I picked this flower*
and *kissed it and put it in this envelope*
    so we could share something tangible
and *hanging onto hope for life*
        and *You're melodramatic and insufferable*
    so meet me in the park at midnight Friday
        tell no one
    and *Is it ok if I still love you more than everyone else*
if I promise not to tell any of them?
        and *You can tell **me***
        and *I was going to leave this on your nightstand*
            but wanted the postman at least

to know you're indulging my hope
                and here are my keys back
                        come home

We take the glue from those hundreds of envelopes
        and we cover ourselves in it
until we pick up shattered laughs
                clinging to our walls
and our carpets
        and our forks
and our bed-sheets
        and our toothbrushes
and we find ourselves stuck
        but not so that we can't move or get away
                but so we won't be apart
    We roll that glue on our tongues
when we begin to forget
    what each other tastes like
and rub it into the ridges of our fingertips
    so we can feel the other's kisses
            on our faces in droughts of affection
            We use it to piece together new hopes
                    built on histories
        to put fragile things
               back together
               and together again

This is the now
            I am loving you in
and even if we've come apart a time or two
the glue of a thousand love letters
is even stronger than the inevitability of magnetism
it's the tangibility of never refusing
        to try

INQUEST

    The color of my skin is not my privilege
that's just eight pounds I wear
        as proof of a history of slavery
            regardless of race
        because every sequence of our DNA
            is but the battle scars of rapes
                and far more brutal reparations
    Specifically
        as a Spaniard
I started out black

        Yes
my people were the Carthaginians
        North Africans racing the Romans for the title
Supreme Murderers of the Mediterranean
    after they annexed Greece
and we harvested the ruins of Persia for spears

    We were stubborn
        so they had to squash us three times
    and by the time they were done with us
        we were white
            Our slaves switched sides
those who escaped back to Africa
            survived with the same skin

but us Spaniards we were stuck
        getting stuck despite our screams

We ran until we settled in the mountains
where we were elated to find Jewish kings in exodus
        Sympathy and a shared history spared us the sadism
                but not the slavery

        We had barely settled in before the Moors —
who were once our brothers —
        came raging across the sea
to see to it we had no peace
        we tried to run deeper into the mountains
            some of us made it
                and became the Portuguese
        but most of us
            were caught and reconverted
they raped us until we turned black again
            they made us scrub our history
        off our holy places
            and for another seven hundred years
        we were slaves and subhumans again

In 1492 when Ferdinand and Isabella
        kicked out the last of the Moors
and set out to making us white again
        we said *never again*
                and set out for South America

That's where it gets strange
>	because you'd think sixteen-hundred years
would have soured us Spaniards on slavery
>	but instead
>	we started an Inquisition at home
>	>	and conquered an entire hemisphere

>	And do you know why?

>	Because it feels good to crack the whip
>	it feels good to be the ones at last
>	holding the women down
>	>	and changing their skin
>	and erasing their history

>	>	But it didn't matter anyway
because damn't history
>	is just slaves hoping and dreaming
>	>	and scheming to enslave their masters

We are all rape victims
>	just as we are all rapists
Rape victims turned rapists at the first opportunity
>	rape victims who raped their rapists
>	>	for a while
before they got raped back again

>	We are damned
so long as we keep thinking justice is revenge

and peace can only be
>in a promised land where providence
grants our chosen people
>all the power and primacy we deserve

I remind you Spain was ripped apart
>and burned and rebuilt
>>over and over
>over which sons of Abraham
>>owned heaven
>and therefore the world

Therefore my privilege
>is not my skin
it's that being born at the right time
in the right place
with the right gods
>means I can admit my people were wrong
>>that my ancestors were monsters
>so savage and sadistic
>they were unsuitable for heavenly souls

and never have to deny that past
>for fear it would risk
my people a better future

CROSSED CRUDE & SO VERY CONFUSED

    Do you find me offensive
        just because I wear lady clothes?
    Because I shave my legs
        because I like eyeliner and lipstick
    and looking like a boy and a girl
        at once
    while feeling the need to be neither?

        It's not the brutally clichéd alcoholism
            the bottoms-up rot gut
straight from the bottle stream of hateful obscenities
    and obsessing about gnostic supremacy
        even at the cost of evenings
            and friendships and memories

  No
      that's all fine

  but fishnet stockings
pink earrings and cutesy pastel t-shirts
      takes it too far?

    So it's perfectly acceptable
to scream down any suggestion of my fallibility
      and plug my ears
            and stick my tongue out

                    but if I paint my nails —
                heaven forbid my toes —
      our ordered society will crumble into chaos
a crime wave will swallow every suburb
        and all the satellites will fall from the sky?

    Ya know
        the only consequences I ever see —
beside you hating yourself for being attracted to me —
        is the bold tickling of boundless curiosities
that makes it easier for the exiled
            to crown their divergences like they were precious
            and be unashamed
of the forbidden treasures of their identities

    So that said
        your worst case scenario WWIV
is that children will start coming to their own conclusions
        and thumbing their noses
            at their parent's ghost stories?!

But no harm no foul
        if I'm louder and more obnoxious than a train horn
            more bloodthirsty and malicious
        than a faith-healing
            polygamist with Ebola

I can mock love and appreciation and tolerance
        I can be an inconsiderate prick

I can have my tongue stuck-on-sour
                like it was a frozen sign pole
        of venom and disparity
        and crack the whip of my cruelty
to keep me safe from the calamity of community

And there is nothing wrong with that

                But I can't call gender roles
        an anachronism of patriarchal power structures
            and let my insides come out
        and giggle like a carefree and innocent princess
              in hopes it inspires
                      abandoned children
                      to feel fine doing the same?

GET FUCKED

You are just a parasitic worm
        building gates and walls and ghettos
and sweatshops and genders
        to confine us to conformity
so you can continue to get off
        with your boots on ascendant hope's throat

Fuck you
        for managing to make my worst
seem like a joke that's less funny
        for being true

GIRLS

               I think deep down
        every man wants to be a seventeen-year-old boy again
because only a fool would relish responsibility

        But shit there you are
growing liver-spots making silly faces
                calling someone in their thirties a girl
because you can't deal with girls being done with you
             and in the end
          you being done with them

              One day
        you're gonna get some woman pregnant
and you're gonna hafta either kill yourself
              or realize your child makes you a man —
whatever the hell that means—

        and you wouldn't really go back
                even if you were given the chance
to relive outrunning your mistakes
        because it was that close of a call
                          and you know it

JUST SAY PLEASE

      The power of praying is in the believing
believing that conjuring miracles is child's play
          when you have a child's perfect faith
that if you cry
     and you beg
and you been a good little girl
     you're gonna get what you want
in god's time

But you must ask
          piously for the proper kind of things
              you must plead from your knees
        facing the right direction and the right symbols
while saying the right words in the right order
       making right on your mamma's instructions
          how to make everything alright

Only by these magic words
        will the heavens open
      in grace to grant you all your greatest hopes —
most especially those that erase the past
         and prevent the future

And the proof of prayer
        is in the believing too
    because when you believe
that someone's listening who can change the things you can't
        it takes away the pain and the pressure
    of wondering what comes next
as well as every second third fourth fifth guess
        you get to believe every tomorrow will be better
because the architect of the universe watches out for you
        which makes your wants blessed

        Believing in prayer
is the antidote for apprehension and guilt

            Apprehension because just by asking
        bad gets better
    and guilt because just by praying
        sins get pardoned
and if god's grace doesn't immediately purify you
        your penance of a few more prayers
            will bring you back in the good graces of god

Of course
    god only answers the prayers he wants to
the right kind you were right to ask for in the first place
        and he's been working on them anyway
            because he knows you
        he made you

he made you imperfect
and your free-will inevitably leads you afoul
in a variety of predictable ways
but he'll fix everything if you just keep asking
and keep the faith

We don't know any better
but to put power in prayer
because what else would we do when we felt helpless
We ask for answers and assistance
non-stop and non-nonsensically
from mere mortal sinner screw ups like ourselves
to occupy the time and vent the stress
of staring down the unknown
for only god knows how long

It only makes sense
to bow our heads and close our eyes
or fold our hands and scan the sky
when believing being part of a plan bigger than ourselves
always makes us feel so much better
So we do
it's inherent in our humanity
to look to the stars
and pray to a god we barely believe in
to fix things when we can't find our answers
and assurances on earth

And good!

Because believing
> in ANYTHING

in any of the millions of gods we've made up
is so much better
than struggling alone
> or taking solace in the love of people
>> who at best
> can only soften the blows

>> The worst part
>> is that in this world with no god
>>> is where we need god the worst

A CRYING SHAME

        Don't worry son
it's not your fault
        that your grandparents keep you a secret
that your only communication
        comes by care package
        and that you can never come to holidays
Son
        this will be the only time in your life where
                It's not you it's me
        will be the truth

        Because it's THEM
                they are the perfect consumers
                      completely consumed
                and afraid of affection
        If you don't feel loved
it's not because you're not worth loving
        but because they don't know how

They make every attempt at kindness
        without any concept of compassion
they want you to be cookie-cutter american dream
        because that's what has made them happy
and love for them is changing people

but there is no changing where you come from
and now that you're six
neither of us need changing

Oh Isaac
I am stubborn like you
so I was resistant
when they chased me
with razor sharp psychological shoehorns
I was defiant when their blessing came with conditions
I've been disowned a dozen times
and I didn't stop wishing they were dead
until I turned twenty-five

I really hope you never feel the same way
but understand that this schism is deep seated
and right now
me and them are many years deep
in a stand-off about when I'll stop cross-dressing
and being a shame to them
so you are only a shame to them because of me
because me and your mother never got married
or ever really liked each-other in the first place
so we never formed the kind of family
they feel comfortable including in their christmas cards

but I don't hold that against you
or even her really

but they'll always hold it against me
>   that I wouldn't deny myself
for their greater glory
>   >   and I think they also hate me
>   for never denying you

>   So I know what it's like
>   wishing for a family
>   >   that wants you
>   >   >   but I want you
>   >   >   and the best I can offer
>   >   is the promise
>   >   that I'll never lie to you like you were stupid
>   >   I'll never deny your self like I knew better
and I'll certainly never force you
>   >   to change for the holidays
>   >   like I wish you were someone else

>   No
I will love you for what you are
>   >   always
>   >   even if you're a christian
>   >   >   even if you are a neatnik normie
>   >   you come to me exactly as you are
and I will parade you in front of my friends
>   >   and not as any proof of me
but because I've always thought you were perfect

        I love you Isaac
    and the only condition of my love
       is that you'll never let anyone make you hate yourself
for what you are

    I know it's hard to hear
but we don't need them
    to be happy

THIS POEM CAN'T GET NO SATISFACTION

This poem is sitting on its front step
searching the clouds for letters
      and punctuation
making paper-mache dolls
      out of obituaries and headlines
in the shape of poems

          It is rummaging
     in the open graves of wastebaskets
         for unsent love letters
              and telephone bills
         that tell it who you've been talking to

    It is listening to the neighbors fight
            to barking dogs
         to talk radio hosts
    and its only companions
           orphaned musical notes
        in search of a song

This poem is strung together
      with bird-nest spit and cigarette cellophane
         it is only the packaging material
    other poems come in

                          This poem is touching itself
and sighing the names of other poems
                it is visiting online thesauri
      like they were dating sites
and studying book covers and paintings
                    like they were pornography

This is the poem
        that cannot write itself
but would like to
        when you are sleeping
despite it being homeless and friendless

This poem is lusting after
        all your unfinished poems

(NOT) GIRLFRIEND

                    Me and my NOT girlfriend
               are NOT obsessed with each other
          we do NOT talk about each other incessantly
or insist on rambling nonsensical strings of vagaries
                    we are NOT disturbing
our sex life has NOT caused
        all my neighbors to move
and we do NOT shamelessly grope each-other in public
                      because that would be tawdry
                                and *rude*

Me and my NOT girlfriend
                are NOT codependent
         we spend at least five days every month apart
                  we HATE snuggling
gratuitous nudity is completely out of the question
              our art is NOT creepily preoccupied
my bedroom walls are NOT covered
             in paintings of our faces
         our poetry is NOT littered with inside jokes

The only reason I'm letting her tattoo all available skin
                  is that I'm cheap

we are NOT splashing in the sick pleasures
of any illusion of permanence

    Me and my NOT girlfriend
        do NOT go on adventures
            or do laundry together
                or ever cook dinner
        We do NOT go shopping
            or spend Sundays in bed
        We do NOT make pit stops for kisses
            share clothes
        or do any goddamn cooing at each-other
            we are not in love

    (ewwww)

    Me and my NOT girlfriend
are NOT even slightly sentimental
    we do NOT have pet names
        we do NOT write love letters
we are NOT crowded by silly dime store trinkets

    We do NOT have matching tattoos
        boots
    women's underwear
        hairstyles
bracelets

                    tastes in breakfast food
or affections for prank calling my landlord

                          She is NOT my soul-mate

                    How could you be so confused
just because I'm fucking my best friend

I DO NOT HAVE A GIRLFRIEND!

SPARROW

    So here I am before you
            like an oppressive neon explosion
that gets children hooked on drugs and bestiality

         And yet
                not even an hour ago
      I was hiding from my neighbors
with my face pressed to the floor behind my door
               and the lights off
        holding my breath
           about to burst into tears

    Because all the locks and hinges and footsteps
           were so loud
                and so close
        I was afraid they might find me
           that my door would open
    that the light would pour in
and that I would find it all staring at me
      compromised and without the charisma
        I characterize as a shield
    and then the world that knows
my more susceptible parts would smile
      the sweetest silent hello

          and I would be lost
for words
          and for further recesses to back into
                    I'd blush
          ashamed
          of all the things I've ever done
so close
          to their happy lives
and I'd wish I was someone else
          and want to leave
                    but find myself
at home

SOLD!

    The body count is getting hard to ignore
and even the law and order republicans
        are acknowledging that so many criminals
are hiding behind their uniforms

    But for every name that becomes a battle cry
thousands upon thousands of quieter crimes
               are committed not by cops
        but in the courts
where there are fortunes being made
putting a million black men back in chains

    Because occupied cells equal dollar signs
           and the new slave masters
       of the for profit prison system
have pierced one-in-thirteen black men with a price tag
          so they can be bought and sold

    The economics of inequality
           revolves around the resource
       of our collective cultivated fear
    fear that we're constantly on the verge
       of being victimized
by a culture of criminals

      and we won't be safe
unless we lock them up on sight

      So we've bought cops
and step one is selling them
          on the concept of the African Savage
              so they don't see citizens but suspects

          So step one complete
            cops bought
      Seventeen-year-old boy in the back of the car
                 ready to be sold
            and charged with a felony
              for walking home
      with dark skin that matches crude descriptions
            of so many suspects
          step two is finding a buyer

      They parade the commodity
in front the judge and the prosecutor
      and since sympathy is superseded
by the promise of profits
          when getting convictions
          feeds the commerce of putting bodies in cages
            simple ruthless bartering begins
      Do I hear Armed Robbery
five to fifteen five to fifteen five to fifteen five to fifteen

Do I got nine?

NINE

Can I get ten?

TEN!

Bleeding on a cop constitutes felony assault right?
Assault on an Officer
one to five one to five one to five one to five

Do I got three?

SOLD!

And the judge slams his gavel
thirteen years behind bars
for an innocent seventeen-year-old boy
isn't of any importance to the people counting their
STACKS of kickbacks

So cops bought
judge and prosecutor happy buyers
the third and final step
is getting the good people —
you and me —
to be complacent consumers
in the economy of inequality
so sold on being scared
we can be counted on to buy

I mean we've been sold the threat of gun violence
so we can buy more guns

                  we've been sold the scourge of drugs
so we get addicted to popping pills by prescription
we have been sold burglar alarms and security guards
       and surveillance cameras and metal detectors
so a million black men in chains
             doesn't seem like slavery
           but is justified for our safety

           But if we didn't buy
if we refused to believe that all black men
             are dangerous animals run amok
constantly committing crimes
           we couldn't be convinced that our communities
               need segregation for security
           and there is no way they could sell us
              on filling up so many cells
           if the story was the 'families people come from'
instead of the 'fiends coming for our families'

           If we didn't buy
               human lives
           wouldn't be for sale

SCAPEGOAT (SILENCING THE LAMB)

HEY DAD

So I'm hanging here
        skewered through my arms and feet
            eight feet up in the air
and every breath hurts more than the last
        mostly because it's occurred to me
that I've been lied to
        and left to die
You don't have a concept of time
        so you're not running late
    you never meant to save me in the first place
        and you only promised angels
    because you knew all along
I'd never go along with it otherwise

It's staggering and sickening to make me
        an unwitting sacrifice

I mean what did you expect?
        YOU ABANDONED THEM
    And now you've abandoned me
because you're so dead set on how shitty everyone is
that I'm in agony over yet to be committed sins

like there was some possible way to please you
>
> you god who defines perfection on the fly

and perfect?

> Your idea of salvation is evidently suicide

and don't think I've forgotten about Isaac and Job
>
>> I mean JOB
>
> You cast lots on our lives
>
>> How many people need to die
>
> before you're satisfied?

> And father

I was doing just fine
>
> literally millions of miracles
>
> to make your creation a better place
>
> but that wasn't making it happen for you
>
>> now was it?

> My mission was never to save anyone

but to save face for you
>
> so you could say
>
>> like some kind of moody teenager
>
> *I tried the best I could to show the world I loved them*
>
>> *so now I'm killing myself*
>
> *so they know how much I cared*

Except even moody teenagers don't think
> their way is the only way

                they know empathy
           is more than empty gestures
                and forgiveness
                    isn't just the warm feeling
of hearing someone admit they were wrong

Even teenagers aren't so vain
                as to insist on believing
          they have nothing to be forgiven for

       So I'd appreciate an apology
It's too late to get me off this thing
       they're about to lance me in the side
because they can't stand to see me suffer anymore
                but it would be nice for you to admit
                    before I suffocate
       that you're mad at me
                  and the whole world
for loving each other more
       than they will ever love you
             and it's not their fault
they've learned to suffer each other
                with GRACE and not vengeance

            I'd like to apologize with my last breath
                for being belligerent
                    but after all

        I'M FUCKING DYING HERE
and the Roman soldiers got me drunk on cheap wine
        so I won't have to endure the agony
    of being forsaken without any solace
and there is no solace in being your lamb
      tricked into the slaughter

I thought I was your bulldog

      I see now
          like every one else ever born
              and everyone that will ever be born
I'm dying as a scapegoat

MY ONE & ONLY HAPPY POEM

    My greatest joy
        is sashaying into a sports bar
    all dolled up
        with elated lipstick smile
            and saddling up
    to the biggest bro there
        and tapping him on the shoulder to say
            Hey yo what's the score?

They always stare at me for a few seconds
    not quite sure what to say
wondering if my curiosity
    is just part of a larger knob gobbling game
like maybe if they answer it'll turn them gay
        so I more often than not
    have to follow up with more specific questions
        so it's clear I'm curious about sports
    and not what they're packing in their pants

Our starting pitcher — Guthrie
    —how uh how's his curve ball working today?
    and the catcher
has he been smart enough to call for low and away
        when we're way ahead in the count?

And then
>their lips and assholes un-pucker

Uh yea man
we got a two-hit shutout going into the fifth inning
and we're up three runs
So I got a question ...
>and I cut him off

I say
Yes I did used to hate my father
but not anymore
and my wife of three years
is probably better in bed than yours
Man when she wraps her legs around my back
it ain't long before we're both screaming CAL RIPKIN
Anyway did you say we're up 3 runs?
Does that mean our power is producing runs
and we're not just swinging at ghosts again?

And that's when my shit-eating-grin
dissolves all boundaries and me and this bro
are just talking about baseball
and the sports we played in high school
and how much we pretend to bench-press
and even if he's still wondering why I'm dressed
like a slutty seventeen-year-old riot grrrrrl
his guard's down
and he's not afraid to introduce me to his friends

            and it doesn't seem so far fetched
that faggots and sports fanatics
      aren't mutually exclusive sects
            What you need to understand
is that I'm not some freedom fighter
I mean I take great pride in knowing
      that the bastillion of machismo has softened
           its membership policies because of me
                but so much more importantly
      it's being able to come out of the closet
            about being a cross-dressing jock
because hating injustice and the New York Yankees
            with the same fire is really lonely
when the creative world
      is so unkind to us athletic queers
artists have told me repeatedly
      and in no uncertain terms
           that I am not allowed to be
all of me all at once
      because it's some arbitrary abomination

So then my greatest joy
      isn't just crushing assumptions
it's living above them
           where all the whys don't matter
      and I'm not explaining myself

cause we're just talking about the game

AN ODE TO MY PRECIOUS UNDERWOOD

      Crawling back to you
            bottle and patient smile
                between open arms
           and quivering butterfly fingers
is something I'm not
    necessarily proud of
        but you fill me with purpose and prancings
so dainty I feel like a enchanted pony
                of perfect possibilities
            kingdoms of giggles
        and unsinkable revelation

           The callous reality
    is that in illusions
        anything is conceivable
                even that things
            will get better
    if I keep you close
            enough to caress
        anytime I have a quiet moment
           and that if I say
every day
        and mean it and keep to it
            and keep searching in you

        I can see gods I don't believe in
and get my merit badges for sacraments
          we're just inventing
        and *lost* will be always
           only a verb

You are a fruitless tour of my interior
        but my home still
     you are a delicate treasure
        proven by loyal lines
            and reliable welcomes

I find you
     most messianic in the dark
        place where future and fortune
and closure and capacity
     snarl over the atria
        of a better tomorrow
waiting for my fingers to trace you
     because you are beautiful in a way
   that my most precise explanations obscure
       by their salty substance

   If you were a saint
you would be the one I prayed to
      for serenity in simplicity

You will always be waiting
                      when I come looking
      with paper and prayers
            that you can pound my anguish
into something pretty

      With you
lost is only
         always
      an affable verb

A FEW LOVE POEMS (PLAUSIBLY) ABOUT JASON RYBERG

JUST ANOTHER 39TH STREET MATTRESS SKIPPER

             We spent spring's lost hour
         telling war stories
   and drinking Boulevard Wheat
         on a moving stage
                          without intermissions
             and I broke character to call you
the best birthday present I'd ever gotten
         cause I meant it more
than my character's coy charade
         and you never ran out
               of beautiful things to say

So
         after kissing you
             more elatedly helplessly and wholeheartedly
than anyone else Mr Rhubarb
         since the last in a long litany
             of illustrious Barons
I elected to stay just far away
             enough from the fountain of your mouth
that I could hear your tongue click with every syllable
         your teeth clack with every emboldened smile
             and your hips swaying
                     and your hands swooping
         while never losing sight of your eyes
until we turned out the lights
         and talked in our sleep
without a blanket
         or any clothes on

         And in the morning you told me
in so many subtle ways to stay

    and I had a hell of a time leaving
      on that street car

Now I'm barely getting home
     to catch the afternoon
   knowing you're hoping
I'll be bothering you soon
    but you'll be waiting at 39th and Bell
when I get off as if to tell me
   no bother please do

STEEL TOE BOOTS MUSE

Long in the tooth
and by that I mean
you talk up a Kansas dust storm
and short on the booze
which means you drank
through Uncle Dwayne's moonshine
before sunset and now you are
kickin clay dirt and loose gravel
walking the fire road up to the cemetery
and your boots are old, friend
used to be mahogany brown till the drought won
and burnished them right down to a god-only-knows
shade of this-shoe-walked-a-long-goddamn-way
and right there in the middle is a bald spot
shining bright silver steel saying

> *I could kick a hole right through you*
> *but it likely ain't gonna happen today*

them boots are leather tough
know a tractor clutch
and a jackhammer in the gut
and laid enough tile
to pave I-70 to Denver and back
and those steel toes be found tapping to the radio
somewhere in the deep country
somewhere in the big city
but the song always goes, man
the song always goes.

I WEAR YOU LIKE A FRESHLY HEALED TATTOO

        I wear you like a freshly healed tattoo
            a piece of infinity
                on mortal canvas

        When they bury me
the mortician will see your colors
            and even if he tries to conceal you
                like a blemish
        beneath every facade there you'll be

        I wear you like a freshly healed tattoo
            I strip down
Baron baby
                in wonder of your luster
            obnoxiously and perpetually

In pondering your permanence
at first my ecstatic affection for your intricate details
                overwhelms every other
        tract of cowboy skin in existence
I forget we began and can only end in tears

        I wear you like a freshly healed tattoo
            now that I'm allowed to get you wet
      we'll stay in the shower for hours
            telling the stories of how we got here

        With you on me
            we're stronger than the lions
      waiting to devour our corpses
            we promise to make them starve
      liver spots will cower in fear

I wear you like a freshly healed tattoo
>> my friends will soon grow tired
> of the opportunities I find
>> to tie you into explanations

You're the deepest beauty
> these last several years of searching
can express standing in front of bookshelves
> I conceded to making you mine
>> so how could I possibly control
> my babbling pride?

> I wear you like a freshly healed tattoo
>> I can no longer scrub you away
> you've settled into the pantheon of my skin

>> I might regret you someday
> I might not adore you upon death
>>> but your mark is made
>> and I'll love you
>>> regardless of resent
>> relentlessly

I wear you like a freshly healed tattoo
> a relic
>> at least worthy of rivaling
> the rest of my holy things

I wear you like a freshly healed tattoo
> my mother won't like you

I wear you like a freshly healed tattoo
> and I will never see myself
or *Paul Jay-son* brandy
the same

RIVERSIDE-SUMMER-STORM-TWIN

When my catastrophe struck,
abject, homeless, buffeted to the quick
I did what any poet worth their salty tears would do:
I invented a new best friend.

I conjured up the best of my most fanciful imaginings
and insurrected a sidekick in the form
of the most easy-going nihilist this side
of the seedier sides of the side-roads
of Kansas wind-mill farms:
he's six foot six foot six and made of rodeo dicks
he's a devil's hodgepodge
of sad songs and laughing gas
and he certainly is the most
beloved man in the universe.

He tattoos under-age orphans
before buying them beer,
rescues kittens from trash-fires
and hound-dogs from puppy mills,
has always got an open door for you,
dirt under his fingernails,
dirt to jaw-bone about
and he doesn't give a flea's itch about trying to fit in
he ignores every last one of you
in this room and this city
until you walk into the bookstore
and wanna talk superheroes.

And I love him.

This Don Quixote is laid-back like a hammock,

afternoon sitting in a slow-moving river
watching the blue egrets singing,
he's armed with a twelve pack,
he has a tan line from sunglasses,
and he knows just how to throw Murphy's stick
so the rapids catch it and it's gonna be
a long while till the dog makes it back
and while he's generally known as the life of the party
it's also true that those who really know him
know he's got a case of the one-who-got-away-blues
and a side-eye on anyone
who doesn't do right by her anyway.

And I invented him
because that's how corner store honest
I'd like a dream to be and that's who
I want to have
when I need someone
to have my back.

www.ingramcontent.com/pod-product-compliance
Lightning Source LLC
Chambersburg PA
CBHW020621300426
44113CB00007B/735